THE **FESTIVE** FOOD OF
America

BY MARTINA NICOLLS

Kyle Cathie Limited

First published in 1991 by
Kyle Cathie Limited
122 Arlington Road
London NW1 7HP
general.enquiries@kyle-cathie.com
www.kylecathie.com

ISBN 1 85626 676 1
ISBN (13-digit) 978 1 85626 676 5

this page Corn field and barn; Craig Tuttle /Corbis
pages 4–5 Jamie Grill/Iconica/Getty Images

Designed by **pinkstripedesign.com**

Photography by **Will Heap**

Illustrations by **Sally Maltby**

Home economy by **Lizzie Harris**

Styling by **Roisin Nield**

Production by **Sha Huxtable & Alice Holloway**

Martina Nicolls is hereby identified as the author of this work in
accordance with Section 77 of the Copyright, Designs and Patents Act 1988.

A Cataloguing in Publication record for this title is available from the
British Library.

Reproduction by Colourscan
Printed and bound in China by SNP Leefung Printers Limited

CONTENTS

NEW YEAR'S DAY

It has been said that the South exists on 'hogs and hominy' and this is largely true. Southern pigs are big and fat and make good bacon, smoked hams and the old pioneer stand-by, salt pork. Hominy, one of the standard breakfast foods of the South, is dried corn kernels boiled in lye, hulled and left whole; 'grits' are ground hominy. Either can be boiled and served hot with butter, syrup or 'grease' (melted bacon fat) or cooled and then fried.

Cornmeal, finely ground dried corn, is versatile and used in both the delicate spoon breads of the Virginia gentry and the rough cracklin' breads and 'hoe cakes' of the countryside. Hoe cakes were made by the field hands on the plantations as they worked in the cotton rows; the workers mixed the cornmeal with hog lard, formed flat cakes from the mixture and slapped them onto their hoe blades to bake over an open fire.

Another traditional country way of baking cornbread is in a cast-iron skillet, which is an old English term for a frying-pan. This gives the bread a crisp bottom crust and a camp fire flavour. Serve it for a 'Good Luck' New Year's Day breakfast as all true Southerners do, hot, straight from the pan, with black-eyed peas and rice and a bowl of boiled turnip greens.

CORNBREAD

50g bacon dripping or butter
140g yellow cornmeal
1 egg
85g plain flour
2 teaspoons baking powder
50ml milk
50ml water
pinch of salt

serves 6

1 Melt the fat in a 23cm skillet (cast-iron frying-pan).

2 Mix together the rest of the ingredients in a bowl, adding a little more water if necessary to make a smooth batter.

3 Pour the mixture into the hot skillet and bake in a preheated oven, 180°C/350°F/gas 4, for 25–30 minutes or until golden on top and shrinking from the sides of the pan.

HOPPIN' JOHN

This rather hearty dish of beans and rice most probably had its origins in the slave cabins of the South Carolina rice plantations that fringed the sweltering coastal marshes. It is, if you like, Soul Food, and as with many foods of humble beginnings it has now become a national treasure. Black-eyed peas are small, cream-coloured beans with a black spot around the waist and a slightly smoky flavour. Southern cooks use salt pork but a good smoked bacon works as well.

225g black-eyed peas, soaked
   overnight in water
1 bay leaf
85g smoked streaky bacon in
   a piece, diced
1 medium onion, chopped
2 garlic cloves, minced
1 red chilli
pinch of thyme
115g long-grain rice
salt and freshly ground black
   pepper to taste

serves 6

1 Drain the peas and put them in a deep saucepan with the bay leaf. Cover with about 2cm cold water and bring to the boil. Simmer for 30 minutes.

2 Meanwhile, fry the bacon in a frying pan until crisp. Remove from the pan and fry the onion, garlic and chilli until soft.

3 After the peas have simmered for 30 minutes, stir all the other ingredients into the pot, checking that there is enough liquid to cook the rice. Southern cooks do it by eye; there should be about 300ml, so add more water as necessary.

4 Cover and simmer gently for 10–15 minutes or until the rice is cooked and the mixture is quite dry. If too much liquid remains, remove the lid and simmer for a minute or two to evaporate it.

MARDI GRAS

'Fat Tuesday', a literal translation of the French, is the day before Ash Wednesday.
It is celebrated in many Catholic countries with carnivals and feasts before the Lenten
fasts begin the next day.

The fine old Creole city of New Orleans on Louisiana's Gulf coast has long been
famed for its annual Mardi Gras celebrations. The joint influences of the original
Spanish settlers and the aristocratic French in the eighteenth century brought the city
its fine architecture and its tradition of the finest foods. The history of slavery in the
South brought to New Orleans a legacy of African cultural mixes that gave the city
its marvellous music. This is the home of Dixieland. The Blues and Jazz were born
here, the spiritual homeland of African American music.

Now, sadly, New Orleans, in many places well below sea level, has been devastated
and all but drowned in the floods following the chaos and destruction of Hurricane
Katrina in September 2005. Bruised but valiant, the city is determined to continue
the tradition of Mardi Gras. The days of revels bring together the different elements
and people that have made this city one of the most exciting and interesting in
America. The indomitable spirit striving to bring this gracious city back to life is
manifest in the energy and determination to make music, dance in the streets and
indulge in the excellent foods, traditional bonnes-bouches, Gumbos, pastries and
cakes for which the city is justly famous. The historic French Quarter, being on
somewhat higher ground, was not as badly damaged as the rest of the city, so
Mardi Gras came again to New Orleans. The bands played, the dancing and
Carnival atmosphere went on loudly and joyfully through the night, the celebrations
a tribute and salute to the city, its stalwart citizens and to the hopes for renewal.

right Mardi Gras, New Orleans; Owaki-Killa/Corbis

KING'S CAKE

To honour the enduring spirit of Mardi Gras, this authentic and still very popular brioche recipe is quoted from the 1922 edition of the *Times Picayune Creole Cook Book* published by that Bible of Creole tradition and reverence, culinary and of course otherwise, the *New Orleans Times Picayune*, still a fine and crusading newspaper. And this is still a fine and quite delicious cake.

2 pounds of the best flour
12 eggs
1 cup of sugar
1 pound of the best butter
½ ounce of yeast
½ ounce of salt
candies to decorate

serves 6

'This is a Creole cake associated with the history of the famous New Orleans carnival celebrated in song and story. The "King's Cake" or "Gateau de Roi" is inseparably connected with the origin of our now world-famed carnival balls. In fact they really spring from the old Creole custom of choosing a king and queen on King's Day, or Twelfth Night..."Le Jour des Rois", as the Creoles term the day. King's day falls on January 6, or the twelfth day after Christmas, and commemorates the visit of the three Wise Men long ago...This day is still even in our time the Spanish Christmas, when gifts are presented in commemoration of the King's gifts. With the Creoles...adopting the Spanish custom, there were always grand balls on Twelfth Night; a king and queen were chosen, and there were constant rounds of festivities, night after night, until the dawn of Ash Wednesday. The interval between January 6, or King's Day and Mardi Gras thus became the accepted Carnival Season.

To make the cake put a pound and a half of the very finest quality flour into a large wooden bread trough. Make a hole in the center of the flour, and put in half an ounce of yeast, dissolved in a little warm water. Add milk or tepid water to make the dough, using milk if you want it to be very rich and delicate.

Knead and mix the flour with one hand, while adding the milk or water with the other. Make a dough that is neither too stiff nor too soft, and when perfectly smooth set it aside to rise in a moderately warm place, covering with a cloth. Remember that if you use milk to make the dough it must be scalded, that is must be heated to the boiling point, and then allowed to grow tepid. Let the dough rise for five or six hours, and, when increased to twice its bulk, mix well with it the reserved half pound of flour, into which has been well sifted the salt. Add six eggs, beaten very light with the sugar and butter, and mix all well together. Kneading lightly with your hands, and adding more eggs if the dough is a little stiff. Then knead the dough by turning it over on itself three times, and set to rise again for an hour. Cover with a cloth.

At the end of this time take it up and work again lightly, and then form into a great ring, leaving, of course, a hole in the center. Pat gently and flatten a little. Have ready a baking pan with a buttered sheet of paper in it, and set the big open roll in the middle. Cover the pan with clean, stiff cloth, and set the cake to rise for an hour longer. When well risen, set in an oven a few degrees cooler than that used for baking bread; let bake for an hour and a half; if medium, one hour, and if very small, a half hour. Glaze the brioche nicely with beaten egg, spread lightly over the top before placing in the oven. Decorate with dragees, caramels etc.'

And that is how it was, then. The modern version does not differ in any important particulars. We have quicker, more reliable yeast and electric mixers in place of many willing hands in the kitchen, otherwise the tradition holds firm. A small ceramic figure of a baby – to represent the Christ Child – is baked inside the cake. The person who finds this talisman in their piece of cake will become King or Queen of the festival and must host the next Mardi Gras party... or so the custom goes. Now the brioche has become more colourful – it is iced in three colours: purple to represent Justice, green is Faith and gold for Power. Thousands of these cakes are greedily consumed during Carnival season. It is said to bring good fortune and prosperity for the coming year.

above Mardi Gras float; Philip Gould/Corbis

OYSTERS CREOLE

During the Carnival, street vendors sell these excellent bonnes-bouches, freshly fried, hot and crisp, to the revellers carousing the streets of New Orleans. Serve with lemon wedges and a piquante sauce.

24 large fresh oysters,
   shucked and drained
1 large egg
225ml milk
pinch of salt
freshly ground black pepper
pinch of cayenne
175g fine dry breadcrumbs
85g butter
85ml olive oil
12 parsley sprigs
lemon wedges

serves 4

left photocuisine/Corbis

1 Pat the oysters dry with kitchen paper.

2 Beat the egg, milk, salt, pepper and cayenne.

3 Spread the breadcrumbs on a plate. Dip the oysters, one by one, into the milk and then gently roll them in the breadcrumbs, patting them with your fingers.

4 Heat the butter and oil in a wide, deep frying pan and drop in the oysters in a single layer. Cook for about 4–5 minutes, turning very carefully, until they are crispy and golden brown.

5 Remove and drain on plenty of ktichen paper.

6 Keep the fat in the pan hot, drop in the parsley sprigs and fry quickly until very crisp but still green. Scatter over the hot oysters and serve at once with lemon wedges.

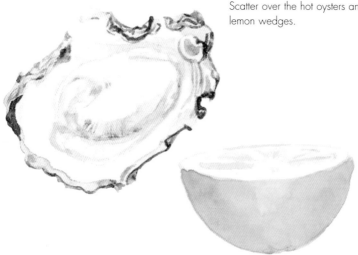

GUMBO

One of the glories of Creole cuisine, Gumbo is a rich blend of fresh shellfish, onions, tiny okra and filé powder, herbs and hot pepper, all combining to great effect in a wonderful thick soup. The curious qualities of okra and filé powder give Gumbo a unique, slightly gluey consistency and sharp/sweet taste. Filé is said to have been manufactured originally by the Choctaw Indians from the tender young leaves of the sassafras tree, which were picked, dried in the sun and pulverised to a fine tilth for cooking and medicinal purposes. It is particular to Creole cooking, and is an acquired taste: use it with discretion. Okra is plentiful throughout the Deep South. Before the introduction of filé powder, okra was the thickening ingredient used in soups and stews. No Gumbo is complete without it. In remote country areas where shellfish is hard to come by, a fine Gumbo is made with chicken, rabbit or squirrel. Gumbo is substantial and needs few embellishments. Serve it in deep soup plates, spooned over a mound of fluffy white rice.

85g plain flour
140g unsalted butter
1 large Spanish onion,
    finely chopped
3 large tomatoes, skinned
    and chopped
450g okra, washed and sliced
    into 1.5cm pieces
a few celery leaves, finely
    chopped
1 bay leaf
sprig of thyme
1 small red chilli, seeds removed
drop of Louisiana hot sauce
    (similar to Tabasco)
225ml bottle clam juice
1.5 litres fish stock
900g cooked prawns, shelled
½ teaspoon filé powder (optional)
small bunch of parsley, finely
    chopped
salt and black pepper

serves 6

1 Spread the flour on a baking tray lined with foil. Bake in a preheated oven, 180°C/350°F/gas 4, stirring occasionally for about 10 minutes or until pale nut brown. Set aside.

2 Heat the butter in a large, deep saucepan. Add the onion and tomatoes, stir briefly, then cover and cook on a low heat for 5 minutes or until the onions are transparent.

3 Add the okra, celery leaves, bay leaf, thyme and chilli and cook, stirring occasionally, for 3 minutes.

4 Sprinkle the browned flour over the mixture. Stir in the hot sauce, clam juice and fish stock. Continue stirring over a medium heat until the mixture is thick and smooth. Bring to the boil, reduce the heat and simmer for 10 minutes.

5 Add the prawns and cook gently for 20 minutes, stirring from time to time.

6 Remove from the heat. Add salt and pepper to taste. Stir in the filé powder and sprinkle with the parsley.

GEORGE WASHINGTON'S BIRTHDAY

As a lad, America's first President was questioned by his father about the chopping down of a favourite cherry tree. Young George, who could have denied all knowledge of this act of infamy, looked his parent straight in the eye and is said to have declared, 'I cannot tell a lie, Father, I cut down the cherry tree.' Having been, no doubt, suitably chastised, the future general and nation's first President was commended for telling the truth.

In Washington's honour, Cherry Cobbler is served every year on the third Monday in February. A delicious pudding, it has a flaky scone-like topping, called a biscuit crust in America. Sour or sweet pitted cherries can be used, although the sour fruit has a truer flavour. To preserve cherries for the winter, little tart ones, much like Morellos, were usually sundried and strung on long threads hanging from beams in cool, dry attics; sweet cherries were bottled or made into jam.

GEORGE WASHINGTON'S BIRTHDAY CHERRY COBBLER

Traditionally made with sour cherries for a sharp taste.
Cobbler is usually served warm with vanilla ice cream.

140g self-raising flour
3½ tablespoons sugar
½ teaspoon baking powder
pinch of salt
100ml double cream
50g unsalted butter, melted
2 x 450g tins sour stoned
  cherries, drained, with 75ml
  cherry juice reserved
1 tablespoon arrowroot
drop of almond extract

serves 6

1 Sift the flour, half the sugar, baking powder and the salt into a bowl. Stir in the cream, mixing well to form a soft dough.

2 Knead on a floured surface for 1 minute. Roll out to 1.5cm thick and cut into six rounds of 6cm diameter. Dip each side in the melted butter and set aside.

3 Mix the cherry juice, remaining sugar, arrowroot and the almond extract in a bowl and stir until dissolved. Add the cherries and pour into a 20 x 20 x 5cm baking tin.

4 Place the rounds of dough, side by side, on top of the cherries. Bake in a preheated oven, 200°C/400°F/gas 6, for 20–25 minutes or until the top is golden and the cherries are bubbling.

ST PATRICK'S DAY

St Patrick's Day, 17th March, is a day of lively celebrations in Boston, New York and Chicago, where the considerable Irish populations have contributed to the character and prosperity of these great cities.

New York has a magnificent parade on Fifth Avenue with pipers, bands and shamrock banners waving. The whole city turns out to stamp and cheer and everyone wears a bit of the 'green'. The many lively Irish bars declare open house; these neighbourhood gathering places are well known for their friendly ambience and good plain food. Of course, on this particular day, there are always traditional Irish specialities chalked on the blackboard and a considerable amount of Irish stew, soda bread and boiled beef is consumed. Carefully made, with a good cut of well-cured meat, boiled beef is excellent eaten hot with mustard, horseradish and pickled beetroot as the traditional relishes. Leftovers can be cut into thin slices for sandwiches.

Mugs of full-strength Irish coffee are a warming and satisfying finish to a cold day's marching in the St Patrick's Day Parade.

top left Marching band in New York City's St Patrick's Day Parade; Ted Russell/ Getty Images
left A man dressed in a St. Patrick's Day outfit gives a 'thumbs up' at a St. Patrick's Day parade on the southside of Chicago; Sandy Felsenthal/Corbis

BOILED BEEF AND CABBAGE

1.8kg salt silverside or
  brisket of beef
1 large onion, peeled and
  stuck with 2 cloves
8 medium potatoes, scraped
  and quartered
8 medium carrots, scraped
  and quartered
1 small swede, peeled and
  cut into thick slices
900g green cabbage, cored
  and quartered
salt and freshly ground
  black pepper

serves 6

1 Soak the meat in cold water for a minimum of 2 hours, and drain.

2 Place the meat in a deep, lidded saucepan, add the onion and enough water to cover them by 2cm. Bring to the boil, skimming off the scum and foam as it rises. Reduce the heat, partially cover and simmer for about $2^1/2$ –3 hours or until the meat is tender.

3 Add the potatoes, carrots and swede and simmer, uncovered, for 20 minutes.

4 If there is enough room in the pan add the cabbage quarters, pressing them into the broth. Otherwise cook the cabbage separately in boiling salted water for about 15 minutes. Add salt and pepper to taste.

5 Remove the meat and vegetables and drain. Slice the beef and arrange on a platter in overlapping slices, surrounded by the vegetables. Serve the broth separately.

SUGARING-OFF

The north-eastern woods and the deep forests around the Great Lakes are sugar maple tree country. Between winter and spring, when it 'isn't too cold and it isn't too warm', the soft Sugar Snow falls, covering young daffodils with a thick, cool carpet. This signals the running of the maple sap, from which maple syrup is made.

In the good old days, before factories and refineries, the trees were tapped with hand-whittled wooden spouts; buckets were hung underneath to catch the thin sap, which was poured into iron cauldrons slung on stout poles between two trees. A crackling hot blaze was stoked through the night and willing neighbours and friends from miles around gathered to join the party and help stir the boiling sap, which had to be watched every minute until it began to thicken (waxing), at which point some of it was poured off into barrels and jugs to keep for syrup. Ladles of the hot liquid were drizzled onto plates of snow to make instant 'taffy' – a huge treat for everyone.

The remainder boiled on until it began to crystallise, when it was quickly transferred to pans to harden into crumbly dark maple sugar. It was a fine occasion for a dance and a local fiddler would play lively reels well into the night at the Sugaring-off party.

MAPLE WALNUT FUDGE

Pure maple syrup makes the richest fudge you can imagine. Make a fairly modest quantity, as a little goes quite a way. A sugar thermometer is a great help and it is probably wise to have one on hand.

500ml maple syrup
175ml double cream
1 teaspoon vanilla extract
115g walnuts, coarsely chopped
walnuts to garnish

makes approx 25 squares

1 Combine the maple syrup and the cream in a heavy saucepan. Stir over a moderate heat until it begins to boil. Continue boiling, without stirring, until a teaspoon of the mixture forms a soft ball when dropped in cold water – 116°C/234°F on a sugar thermometer.

2 Remove at once from the heat and cool to lukewarm – 45°C/110°F – without stirring. Then beat the mixture until it thickens and loses its gloss.

3 Add the vanilla and nuts, and continue beating until creamy. Pour into a lightly buttered shallow tin, 20cm square.

4 Leave to cool in the tin. Mark into squares before the fudge is completely cold and garnish with a walnut on top of each square.

A QUILTING BEE

In spring, all over America, ladies gathered for Quilting Bees – days when they would work together assembling and finishing their quilts. It was also a splendid excuse for chattering and exchanging news after a long winter.

The 'pieced tops' or patchworks were stretched onto sturdy frames to be lined, backed and finely quilted before they could be used. A good quilter was famed for her matching of pattern and colour and, of course, the invisibility of her tiny stitches. In Mormon Utah, Quilting Sisters travelled to remote homesteads helping out with the quilting in exchange for room and board. No doubt they also brought longed-for company and gossip as well as quilting news.

Many quilts have been identified as coming from particular communities; Amish-Pennsylvania Dutch work is easily recognised by its plain geometric design and very bold use of colour, red in particular.

Quilting was a community affair, and hungry work. The industrious ladies would stop for light refreshment, home-baked cakes with perhaps some fresh buttermilk poured from cool earthen jugs. A lady, after all, was judged on the quality of her baking as critically as on the finesse of her quilting.

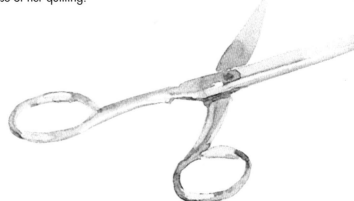

QUILTER'S CAKE

In the 1880s, a Minnesota farmer's wife mentions in her diary tasting a brown sugar pound cake at a neighbour's Quilting. Whilst white sugar was expensive and difficult to come by, on most farms there would always be good milk, butter and eggs and, sometimes, a fine nut tree in the yard.

450g self-raising flour
½ teaspoon baking powder
large pinch of salt
170g butter, softened
170g vegetable margarine
450g light brown sugar
5 large eggs
250ml milk
1 teaspoon vanilla extract
170g walnuts (or pecans),
   chopped

makes approx 25 squares

1 Sift the flour, baking powder and salt. In an electric mixer cream the butter and margarine until light and add the brown sugar and beat until fluffy.

2 Beat in the eggs one at a time, and add the flour mix alternating with the milk. Blend well and stir in the vanilla and nuts.

3 Pour into a well-greased 25cm tube tin or a 900g loaf tin and bake in a preheated oven, 160°C/ 325°F/gas 3, for 1½ hours or until the cake begins to shrink from the sides and the top springs back when lightly pressed. Leave in the tin for 20 minutes then turn out onto a wire rack to cool.

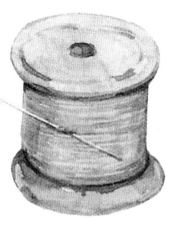

THE KENTUCKY DERBY

Since 1875 the first Saturday in May
has seen sleek three-year-old
thoroughbred colts and fillies assemble
at Louisville's Churchill Down
Racecourse for the running of the
Kentucky Derby, America's most
prestigious and famous race.

It is one of the great social events of
the year, and the even sleeker
racegoers come from all over the
world. Traditionally the day begins
early with elegant breakfasts at the
grandest homes and horse farms in
the county, where Kentucky cured
hams baked to a mahogany polish,
tender, hot Cream Biscuits and Mint
Juleps are served to start a glorious
day of racing and socialising.

right Kentucky Derby Victory 1988; Bettmann/Corbis

BOURBON BAKED HAM

In Kentucky hams are smoked over hickory chips to give a delicate flavour to the meat. They are then glazed and baked to a crisp savoury-sweet finish and can be served hot or cold.

1.8kg smoked gammon joint
250ml Bourbon whiskey
115g dark, bitter marmalade
1½ tablespoons strong mustard

serves 8

1 Place the gammon joint in the centre of a double piece of tinfoil large enough to enclose the joint completely.

2 Mix the Bourbon, the marmalade and the mustard to make a glaze and spoon over the gammon. Wrap the meat in the foil to make a parcel, folding and pinching the edges tightly.

3 Bake in a preheated oven, 190°C/375°F/gas 5, for 1½ hours.

4 Remove from the oven (but do not turn it off). Carefully open the foil and allow the meat to cool for 5–10 minutes. With a sharp knife cut away the rind to leave a 1cm layer of fat. Score the fat into squares and spoon the baked glaze over the surface, making sure the fat is well covered.

5 Leaving the foil open, return the gammon to the oven and continue cooking, basting frequently, for about 30 minutes or until the glaze turns crisp and dark brown.

6 There will be plenty of gravy left from the glaze. Pour off as much fat as possible and serve the gravy separately.

CREAM BISCUITS

No Derby breakfast is complete without a plate of hot buttered 'biscuits', which are similar to English scones but lighter and flakier. In the days of the old South, plantation cooks would beat the biscuit dough with a flat wooden mallet for half an hour to make them tender and light. Since the advent of baking powder in the late nineteenth century, biscuits are less violently and more quickly made, but just as excellent. Serve them straight from the oven, split in two and spread with honey butter.

285g self-raising flour
1 teaspoon salt
½ teaspoon baking powder
1½ tablespoons caster sugar
250ml double cream
115g unsalted butter, melted

makes 12

1 Sift the dry ingredients into a bowl and stir in the cream, mixing well to form a soft dough. Turn out and knead on a floured surface for about 1 minute. Gently roll the dough to 2cm thick and cut into 5cm rounds.

3 Dip each side of the rounds in the melted butter and place on an ungreased baking tray.

4 Bake in a preheated oven, 200°C/400°F/gas 6, for 15 minutes, until puffed and pale golden.

HONEY BUTTER

115g unsalted butter, softened
115g thick honey
1 teaspoon grated orange rind

1 Beat all the ingredients together until fluffy.

MINT JULEP

1 teaspoon caster sugar
6–8 fresh mint leaves
115g crushed ice
85ml Kentucky Bourbon

serves 1

1 Crush the sugar and mint leaves in a glass and stir in some of the ice.

2 Mix in the Bourbon.

3 Pour the mixture into a frosted tumbler and fill to the brim with the remaining ice. Decorate with a mint leaf or two.

FOURTH OF JULY PICNIC

Independence Day, 4th July, commemorates the adoption by the Continental Congress of the Declaration of Independence in 1776. This document gave the American people the right of government by choice, and the resulting hard-fought Revolutionary war between England and Colonial America consolidated this freedom. Picnics, fireworks, rodeos and even log-pulling races are part of the nationwide celebrations. Every village and town puts out flags and cranks up the band. Farmers in the rich Midwest farm country of central Indiana still think a Fourth of July Picnic without Fried Chicken, lemonade and Grandma's Cream Pie would be unconstitutional.

INDIANA CREAM PIE

A rich, satin-smooth pie which is heavenly topped with sliced fresh peaches or blueberries.

170g shortcrust pastry
115g unsalted butter
85g sugar
500ml double cream
1½ tablespoons cornflour
½ teaspoon vanilla extract
grated nutmeg

serves 6

1 Roll out the pastry to 5mm thick and line a 21cm flan tin. Cover the base with a piece of tinfoil, fill with dried beans and bake blind in a preheated oven, 200°C/400°F/gas 6, for 15 minutes. Reduce the heat to 180°C/350°F/gas 4, remove the beans and foil and bake for a further 20 minutes, until golden brown.

2 Melt the butter with the sugar and 400ml of the cream in a double boiler.

3 Mix the cornflour with the remaining cream and vanilla, stir into the hot cream and cook gently, whisking constantly, for 2–3 minutes until very thick.

4 Pour the filling into the pie shell, grate nutmeg over the top and bake at 200°C/400°F/gas 6 for 5 minutes. Cool on a rack and serve cold.

left Fireworks above the Statue of Liberty, New York City; Ted Russell/Getty Images

FRIED CHICKEN

Serve fried chicken cold and eat it with your fingers, plain and
unadorned but for a sharp mayonnaise and salt and pepper.

1.8kg free-range chicken, jointed
1 egg, beaten
juice of 1 lemon
300ml milk
115g plain flour
paprika to taste
sunflower oil, for frying
1 bay leaf
salt and freshly ground
   black pepper

serves 6

1 Put the chicken pieces in a bowl. Beat the egg with the
lemon juice and milk and pour over the chicken. Marinate
for 30 minutes.

2 Meanwhile, mix the flour, salt, pepper and the paprika
in a sturdy paper bag. Drain the chicken, put a few
pieces at a time in the paper bag, hold the edges firmly
together and shake well to coat the chicken. Continue
with the remaining pieces.

3 Heat about 2.5cm oil in a wide, heavy frying pan.
When hot but not smoking, add the bay leaf and
chicken pieces, skin-side down, and fry over a medium
heat until golden and firm. Turn with tongs and brown the
other side.

4 Lower the heat and fry for about 20 minutes, turning
once more, until the chicken is cooked through, golden
brown and crusty.

5 Drain on crumpled kitchen paper and leave to cool.

SHAKER STRAWBERRY FEAST

The Shakers were disciples of Mother Ann Lee, an English immigrant to America in 1774, who was regarded by her thousands of followers as the female reincarnation of Christ. The Shakers, an off-shoot of the Quaker sect, took their name from the religious ceremony in which they danced, 'shaking out' their sins and refreshing their spirits. The rules were austere: a shunning of artifice and embellishment, common ownership of goods and, it must be said, equal rights for women. These self-sufficient communities lived a celibate life and relied on converts – not surprisingly they are now virtually extinct. Communities, such as Hancock in Massachusetts, were primarily agricultural, although they also sold household implements, farm tools and furniture of simple, functional design and excellent workmanship. The Shakers were in many ways austere but their food was rich with their abundant crops of fruit and vegetables. They were noted for their hospitality to travellers and those fallen on hard times. The Hancock Shaker Village is now a museum. Diaries and letters mention the celebration of an annual strawberry shortcake meal at the peak of the picking season in mid-July, when quantities of this delicious pudding were consumed with great delight.

right A laundry and machine shop dating from around 1790, in the Hancock Shaker Village; Robert Harding World Imagery/Corbis

STRAWBERRY SHORTCAKE

225g plain flour
1 tablespoon sugar
3 teaspoons baking powder
pinch of salt
115g butter
175ml milk
575ml double cream,
  whipped
500g strawberries (or as many as
  you like)

serves 6

1 Sift the flour, sugar, baking powder and salt into a bowl. Add 85g of the butter, rubbing it in with your fingers to a fine crumble.

2 Add the milk and mix it lightly with a fork to make a soft dough.

3 Roll out the dough onto a floured surface to 1cm thick. Cut into six rounds with an 8cm cutter.

4 Transfer to a lightly greased baking tray. Melt the remaining butter and brush the rounds lightly. Bake in a preheated oven, 220°C/425°F/gas 7, for 12 minutes or until crusty brown.

5 To serve: split the hot shortcakes in two and brush with melted butter. Place half a shortcake on a plate, top with strawberries and a big spoonful of the cream. Cover with the other shortcake half, and decorate with more strawberries and whipped cream.

In California's fertile heartland lies Gilroy, the fragrant centre of the state's garlic growing and processing industry. Aside from the massive quantities of the 'scented pearl', California grows marvellous vegetables and fruit such as avocados, citrus and soft fruits and has, through the good works of the many restaurateurs and chefs, spearheaded the revolution in American cuisine. The climate varies from desert to cool forest, with the rolling hills of the Napa and Sonoma valleys to the north of San Francisco producing some of the finest wines in the world. These elements combine to make California a place of gastronomic pilgrimage for Americans and Europeans alike – the food is fresh and light, the produce local and the blending of flavours and ingredients reflects the many cultural influences of the American West. American cooking has taken on a new spirit and direction under the Californian sun.

Over twenty five years ago the town of Gilroy declared a festival to pay homage to garlic. This aromatic three-day event is a veritable extravaganza with every possible use and adjunct of garlic being displayed. It was here, apparently, that garlic ice cream was first invented. And it is here that one can buy anything and everything to do with garlic. The air is thick with the pungent aroma – Will Rogers, the home-spun American humorist, described Gilroy as 'the only town in America where you can marinate a steak by hanging it on the clothes line'.

left Gilroy, garlic capital of the world billboard; Kevin Schafer/Corbis

AVOCADO GARLIC SOUP

This delicate cold soup is best made with fresh young garlic and ripe but firm avocados. In California avocado trees grow in abundance and many a back yard will have its own proud tree dripping with fruit. The young purple-green garlic is almost sweet with a sharp edge that does not offend the mellow avocado. Fresh juicy limes are also plentiful in California and can be picked off the tree outside the back door. Serve in small white porcelain bowls.

1 litre chicken stock, degreased
4 fresh young garlic cloves,
   peeled and chopped
2 medium avocados, skinned
   and diced
juice of 1 lime
salt and freshly ground
   black pepper
fresh coriander leaves to garnish

serves 6

1 Combine all the ingredients and blend in a food processor, in batches, until satin smooth.

2 Adjust the seasoning to taste. Chill for at least 2 hours. Pour into individual soup bowls and decorate with coriander leaves.

INDIAN ARTISTS' MARKET

Santa Fe, New Mexico, is Spain's old colonial capital. Founded in 1610, it is a timeless and mellow place, where the sun is bright and hot and the air cooled by mountain breezes. Fiestas and markets take place throughout the year with the Indian Artists' Market in mid-August as one of the most colourful and popular art fairs of the summer.

More than 500 of the South-West's American-Indian artists bring their work to be judged in competitions and sold in a lively street market. It packs the city's tree-lined square and twisting adobe streets. The quality and variety of the hand-woven rugs and baskets, traditional pottery, kachina dolls, drums and astonishing sand paintings are shown in the number of buyers who flood the streets from dawn onwards.

During the day there are feasts of specially prepared Indian foods and stalls selling wonderful spicy-hot snacks of Indian Fry Bread and hot Chilli Sauce. The food in Santa Fe strongly reflects the two cultures that have influenced the South-West: Indian and Spanish; and the ingredients – corn, squashes, chilli peppers, pumpkin, piñon nuts and beans – are all native to the land.

left Chilli peppers; Stuart Westmorland/Corbis

INDIAN FRY BREAD

Fry Bread is an Indian staple. Easy to make, the fried rounds of bread are crisp and golden on the outside and light and soft within. They are delicious split open and served warm with butter and wild honey. For picnics eat them cold sandwiched together with cream cheese and chopped fresh chives, or with a sharp Chilli Sauce (see page 53).

225g self-raising flour
1½ teaspoons baking powder
pinch of salt
1 tablespoon olive oil
250ml warm water
sunflower oil for frying

makes about 20

1 Sift the flour, baking powder and salt into a large bowl.

2 Pour in the oil and water and mix to a soft dough.

3 Knead on a floured surface for about 1 minute. Pat into a 1cm thick round and set aside, covered, for 20 minutes.

4 Shape into balls about the size of an egg. Pat flat and poke a hole through the centre with your finger.

5 Heat 5cm of sunflower oil in a deep, medium-sized saucepan until hazy. Fry the dough in batches, four or five at a time, for about 5 minutes, turning often, until golden brown.

6 Remove with a slotted spoon and drain on kitchen paper.

CHILLI SAUCE

The variety of chilli peppers is wondrous. Green, red and orange, they can be fiery, unbelievably fiery, or even sweet and mild. Individually, red and green chillies are made into sauces to be served 'on the side' with virtually all meats, grains and beans. If you prefer your chilli sauce over the food ask for it to be served 'like Christmas' with the red and green sauce dolloped side by side on the top.

This fresh chilli sauce can be served hot or cold and is particularly good as a topping for cornbread or vegetable bakes. If you have the digestion of a cast-iron boiler, double the quantity of chillies and do not discard the seeds.

2 tablespoons olive oil
5–6 fresh green chillies,
   either hot or mild, deseeded
   and finely chopped
1 medium onion, finely chopped

2 large tomatoes, finely chopped
2 garlic cloves, minced
1 tablespoon cider vinegar
salt

makes enough
for 20 Indian Fry Breads

1 Heat the oil in a frying pan and add the chillies, onion, tomatoes, garlic and vinegar.

2 Sauté the mixture until the liquid has evaporated and the vegetables are just tender. Add salt to taste.

CORN AND CHEESE PUDDING

A Navajo savoury pudding similar to cornbread but richer and substantial enough for a light luncheon or supper dish. Serve it hot, cut into thick slices, topped with a fiery Chilli Sauce (see page 53).

350g tin corn kernels, rinsed
and drained
175ml milk
225g yellow cornmeal
75ml olive oil
½ teaspoon baking powder
2 large eggs, well beaten
½ teaspoon salt
3 fresh green chillies,
deseeded and chopped
100g Cheddar cheese, grated

serves 6

1 In a large bowl mix the corn and milk. Add the cornmeal and olive oil and stir well.

2 Stir in the baking powder, eggs and salt. Mix in the chillies and cheese.

3 Pour into a greased, deep glazed earthenware baking dish and bake in a preheated oven, 200°C/400°F/gas 6, for about 35 minutes or until slightly browned on top and a knife inserted in the centre comes out clean.

HATCH CHILLI FESTIVAL

Chillies are New Mexico's biggest cash crop and Hatch is the state's chilli-growing capital. Every year on Labor Day an annual chilli festival is held in the hangar at the local airport, and this jolly occasion celebrates every conceivable use of the ubiquitous vegetable, with cookery competitions, carnival rides, cook-outs and barbecues and the crowning of the Chilli Queen. Everyone wears Western hats and cowboy boots and avidly discusses the best way to make chilli con or without carne. This is a cause of great rivalry between states, with Texans declaring theirs to be the best – a statement disputed by everyone else in the South-west.

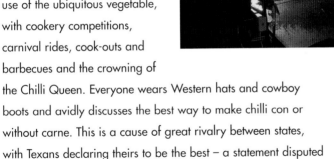

above Man cooking green chillies at the Hatch Chilli Festival; Catherine Karnow/Corbis

left Cooking *Chile Rellenos* at the Hatch Chilli Festival; Catherine Karnow/Corbis

The one fact generally accepted is that beans are *not* cooked with chillies and meat. Beans are served on the side and 'that is that' said a Texan friend. Only Easterners or, worse still, Californians, would think of messing up a good Bowl of Red. After that it is up to you to decide if you prefer chillies fresh or dried, prepared chilli powder or home-made, minced meat or finely chopped beef or pork or even whether or not to add tomatoes – just don't add beans!

CHILLI CON CARNE

What we know as Chilli con Carne is a development of a Native American tribal stew of hot peppers and vegetables. Nowadays incorporating meat, a Bowl of Red, as it is called in the South-west, is basic, beautiful and either fiery or mellow. Cook the chilli the day before you want to serve it, as it improves with reheating. Serve in deep bowls with, for those who insist on fancy trimmings, some finely chopped onion, grated Cheddar and sour cream to stir into the brew.

1½ tablespoons olive oil
1 medium onion, finely chopped
2 garlic cloves, minced
6–8 fresh green chillies, deseeded
   and cut into thin strips
1kg stewing beef or pork, diced
1 tablespoon plain flour
1–1½ tablespoons chilli powder,
   according to taste
1 teaspoon ground cumin
3 large tomatoes, chopped
water
small bunch of fresh coriander,
   finely chopped
salt and freshly ground
   black pepper

serves 6

1 Heat the oil in a heavy casserole and add the onion, garlic and chillies. Sauté gently until softened.

2 Remove the vegetables from the pot, add the meat and brown it well. Add the flour and stir to coat the meat. Add the chilli powder and cumin and cook for a minute or two, stirring constantly.

3 Stir in the tomatoes and onion-chilli mixture. Pour in enough water to just cover the meat. Bring to the boil, then cover and simmer very slowly for about 2½–3 hours or until the sauce has reduced and thickened, the vegetables have almost disintegrated and the meat is very tender. Season with salt and pepper and sprinkle over the coriander.

LABOR DAY

The first Monday in September, Labor Day, is a national holiday, honouring all the workers of America. It is the American version of the European May Day, without the anthropological associations. Traditionally this is the last day of the summer holidays, before going back to work and back to school, and it is celebrated all over the country, with picnics, country fairs, barbecues and bake-outs.

In true North-east Yankee fashion, the people of Bridgehampton, a seaside summer retreat for New York's glitterati, send off the summer with a Clam and Lobster Bake. Long trestles are set in the shade of old oaks, chilled jugs of the local excellent Chardonnay are in plentiful supply and steamed shellfish are heaped on large platters with melted butter and lemon juice. It is wonderfully messy and sublime eating. Though purists insist this should take place on the beach, ideally at twilight with sea-water-filled cauldrons and fires of driftwood, a Clam and Lobster Bake can taste just as wonderful in a summer garden.

CLAM AND LOBSTER BAKE

serves 6

This impressive dish is made by building up alternate layers of ingredients and fresh seaweed. Don't worry if clams are not available; it will be equally good without them.

Take an enormous stew pot, about 9-litre capacity, and, using plenty of very fresh seaweed, proceed thus in layers: cover the bottom of the pot with seaweed, lay on top 4 Quahog clams (very large molluscs), used for flavouring the broth, add another layer of seaweed and cover with 6 scrubbed baking potatoes left whole. Then add another layer of seaweed, 6 chicken quarters, more seaweed, 6 sweetcorn in the husks with the silk carefully extracted, even more seaweed, 1kg live littleneck clams, washed and de-sanded, a final layer of seaweed and, to finish off the pot, 6 x 675g live lobsters.

Pour about 575ml fresh water into the pot. Cover tightly and steam over a medium heat for 45–60 minutes. Remove the lobsters to a platter, and keep warm. Cook the rest a further 20 minutes or until the chicken and potatoes are tender. Discard the Quahogs and the seaweed and pile everything else onto separate platters. Provide crackers for the lobsters, plenty of lemon wedges, melted butter to dip the food into and piles of paper towels to tuck under chins.

BLUEBERRY CAKE

Blueberries are a native fruit in the United States, originally found growing in the scrubby, sandy soil around the north-east coast from July through to mid-September. Now they are cultivated commercially to satisfy the almost infinite American appetite for blueberry desserts, muffins and cakes. This good, moist cake with a crumble topping is an essential finish for a Clam and Lobster Bake.

150g self-raising flour
50g sugar
pinch of salt
2 large egg yolks
50ml milk
50g unsalted butter, melted
175g blueberries
squeeze of lemon juice

CRUMB TOPPING
25g sugar
25g plain flour
25g butter
pinch of cinnamon

serves 6

1 Sift the flour, sugar and salt into a bowl. Stir in the egg yolks, milk and melted butter. Beat vigorously until blended.

2 Line a 20cm square cake tin with greaseproof paper and grease it thoroughly. Spread the mixture evenly, scatter the blueberries over the top and add a squeeze of lemon juice.

3 To make the crumb topping, combine the sugar, flour, butter and cinnamon and work into a fine crumble with your fingers. Sprinkle evenly over the blueberries.

4 Bake in a preheated oven, 180°C/350°F/gas 4, for 30 minutes or until a knife inserted into the centre of the cake comes out clean. Serve warm with vanilla ice cream.

left Blueberry Harvest; David H Wells/Corbis

FESTIVAL OF SAN GENNARO

The patron saint of Naples travelled quite happily to the streets of Little Italy in New York where he is as revered as in the noisy alleys of his home town. San Gennaro came to New York with the Neapolitans who settled in the prosperous New World towards the turn of the nineteenth century. But his history goes further back, to the waning days of the Roman Empire, under the desperate reign of the Emperor Diocletian. San Gennaro, then a Bishop in the early and much-persecuted Christian Church, was tormented and martyred for his beliefs. His remains were gathered by devout followers and brought to Naples where they caused many miracles over the centuries. A relic of the revered saint is carried in procession through the streets of Little Italy as it has been in Naples since time immemorial.

In the ten-day Feast period in mid-September the entire neighbourhood turns out to celebrate with food, music, religious processions and solemn Masses. The excellent restaurants, coffee houses and shops put up decorations, set tables and stalls in the street, and a fine time is had by all. One of the great inventions of the local Italian delis (and now a national byword for over-indulgence) is the Hero Sandwich. It needs an appetite of heroic proportions to eat one. Basically a very long French loaf is split and filled thickly with any combination of Italian salamis, salad, spicy sausage, tomatoes or tomato sauce, meatballs, fried peppers and mozzarella or sharp provolone cheese, or whatever you fancy. A Hero can be ordered up to 130cm in length and could feed a small army.

right Chuch decorated for the San Gennaro festival; Farrell Grehan/Corbis

HERO SANDWICH

30cm French loaf,
   split horizontally
2 tablespoons olive oil
freshly ground black pepper
2 large tomatoes, thinly sliced
115g mozzarella, thinly sliced
50g Italian salami, thinly sliced
1 large red pepper, deseeded
   and cut into strips
50g prosciutto, thinly sliced
50g sundried tomatoes in oil,
   drained
a few fresh basil leaves
a few capers

serves 2–4

1 Lay the split halves side by side. Drizzle the olive oil evenly along the cut surface of both halves and season with pepper to taste.

2 Layer the remaining ingredients in the order listed along the bottom half of the loaf. Top with the other half and firmly but gently press onto the filling, being careful not to squeeze it out the sides.

3 Cut into four thick slices and eat at once or wrap in foil and chill until needed.

HARVEST SUPPER

On the South Dakota prairies, the Harvest Supper was an annual event for homesteaders who attended church for a rousing sermon, to give thanks for the harvest and enjoy the hearty frontier fare contributed by the ladies of the county.

VINEGAR PIE

Pioneer families travelled west with a good supply of sturdy vinegar barrels. Vinegar was used for cleaning pots, as a mild antiseptic, a preservative of foods and as a substitute for lemons, which were as scarce as hen's teeth.

170g shortcrust pastry
225g caster sugar
50ml plain flour
pinch of ground mace
pinch of cinnamon
175ml water
1½ tablespoons cider vinegar
75g butter, melted
2 large eggs, beaten

serves 6

1 Roll out the pastry on a lightly floured surface to 5mm thick and line a 21cm flan tin. Prick the base with a fork and bake blind in a preheated oven, 190°C/375°F/gas 5, for 15 minutes. Turn down the oven to 180°C/350°F/gas 4.

2 Mix the sugar, flour and spices in a bowl. Stir in the water, vinegar and butter and beat in the eggs.

3 Pour the mixture into the pie shell and bake for 30–35 minutes until puffed and golden.

4 The filling will settle as it cools; slice when cold.

left South Dakota prairie church; Dave G. Houser/Post-Houserstock/Corbis

PHEASANT BAKE

4 pheasants
6 thick slices of brown bread,
  toasted
150g butter, plus extra for
  greasing
1 medium onion, chopped
2 stalks of celery, finely
  chopped
115g mushrooms, finely sliced
2 sage leaves, crumbled
575ml chicken stock
50g flour
sprig of thyme
250ml single cream
90g fresh breadcrumbs
salt and freshly ground black
  pepper to taste

serves 10

1 Roast the pheasants in a preheateed oven, 200°C/400°F/
gas 6, for 45 minutes. Strip off the flesh and chop roughly.

2 Crumble the toast into a bowl and set aside. Heat 50g
butter in a frying pan and sauté the onion, celery and
mushrooms until tender. Add the sage, season and remove
from the heat.

3 Pour half the chicken stock onto the crumbled toast, stir in
the vegetables and leave for about 10 minutes. Spread the
mixture over the base of a buttered, deep ovenproof dish and
arrange the pheasant pieces on top.

4 Melt 50g butter and blend in 50g flour with the thyme.
Cook gently, stirring constantly until pale golden. Add the
remaining chicken stock and the cream and whisk over
a medium heat until thick and smooth. Season with salt
and pepper.

5 Pour the sauce over the pheasant and vegetables, scatter
the breadcrumbs on top and drizzle with the remaining butter
(melted). Bake in the oven at 180°C/ 350°F/gas 4. Serve
piping hot.

HALLOWEEN

All Hallows' Eve, 31st October, is the night witches fly on broomsticks across the moonlit sky, Jack-o-Lanterns (hollowed-out pumpkins with grinning, demonic faces lit by candles) flicker mysteriously in dark windows and children all over America dress in spooky costumes and frightening masks. They go from house to house asking for 'Trick or Treat' – a custom evolving from pagan Celtic fire festivals to frighten away evil spirits and souls returning from the dead, and to appease the supernatural powers whose sinister influence controlled the forces of nature. These pagan rituals eventually became secularised, and developed into children's games. They were probably brought to America by immigrants, particularly the Irish in the late nineteenth century. A treat is asked for or a trick is played. Bags of sweets and cookies are quite acceptable and if not forthcoming the wicked witches' curse will descend upon the house and its unfortunate occupants. The evening usually ends with ghost stories around a bonfire and mugs of hot Pumpkin Soup.

PUMPKIN SOUP

Pumpkins were introduced to the early settlers by Indian tribes and are traditionally made into pies and soups. This is a beautifully coloured soup.

1 large orange pumpkin
1kg piece of pumpkin, cut
  into chunks
1 medium onion, finely chopped
small bunch of spring onions,
  finely chopped
3–4 celery leaves, finely chopped
1 garlic clove, minced
85g butter
1.6 litres chicken stock
350ml single cream
1 tablespoon chopped parsley
225g croûtons
salt and freshly ground black
  pepper

serves 8–10

1 Slice the top off the pumpkin to make a lid, scrape out the seeds and stringy bits and carefully scoop out 1kg of flesh for the soup. (Use a separate piece of pumpkin if you prefer.)

2 Sauté the onion, spring onions, celery leaves and garlic in 50g of the butter until tender but not brown.

3 Add the pumpkin chunks and cook gently for 10 minutes. Add the stock and simmer, stirring until the pumpkin is tender, about 15 minutes.

4 Remove from the heat and purée in a food processor until smooth. Return to the pan, whisk in the cream and remaining butter and heat thoroughly without boiling. It should be satin smooth. Add salt and pepper to taste.

5 Warm the hollowed-out pumpkin in a preheated oven, 180°C/350°F/gas 4, for 15 minutes. Pour in the hot soup, sprinkle with parsley and serve the croûtons separately. Or, if preferred, serve in bowls.

The Festive Food of America

PICKING PIÑON NUTS

Piñon (or pine) nuts are gathered in November around Santa Fe. According to local custom, everyone enjoys an energetic day out in the crisp air trooping into the mountains to the piñon and juniper forests to harvest the tiny nuts, which are found in the hard central core of the pine cones and can be notoriously difficult to crack open.

Unless carefully stored – preferably in the freezer – piñon nuts go rancid very quickly. New Mexicans use them throughout the year in breads, cookies, vegetable and meat dishes.

SPINACH AND PIÑON NUTS

This recipe is from Spanish colonial days and can also be made with Swiss chard or dandelion leaves or any combination of the three. The result has an earthy flavour that goes well with grilled meat and game.

550g leaf spinach, washed
3 tablespoons olive oil
1 tablespoon piñon nuts
1½ tablespoons raisins
2 garlic cloves, minced
pinch of cayenne
salt and freshly ground
   black pepper

serves 4

1 Put the spinach in a deep saucepan, cover and cook for about 5 minutes or until tender. Drain thoroughly and chop coarsely.

2 Heat the oil in a heavy frying pan, add the nuts, raisins and the garlic. Sauté gently until the nuts and the garlic begin to colour. Do not let them burn.

3 Add the cooked spinach and heat through until the oil is absorbed. If it seems too dry, add a bit more oil.

4 Season with salt, pepper and cayenne to taste.

FEAST DAY COOKIES

The Pueblo Indians make these crisp cookies for Feast Days and celebrations. The cookies keep well in an airtight tin and are wonderful dipped in hot coffee.

225g unsalted butter
115g sugar
140g wholemeal flour
285g self-raising flour
1 teaspoon baking powder
pinch of salt
100g piñon nuts
100ml water
3 tablespoons sugar
1 teaspoon cinnamon

makes about 48 cookies

1 Beat the butter and sugar until light and fluffy.

2 Combine the wholemeal flour, self-raising flour, baking powder and salt, and gradually incorporate into the butter and sugar, beating well.

3 Mix in the nuts and stir in the water gradually, to form a stiff non-sticky dough. Wrap the dough in clingfilm and chill for 30 minutes.

4 On a floured surface roll the dough 1cm thick. Cut into rounds 2.5cm in diameter.

5 Blend the sugar and the cinnamon and coat each cookie. Arrange on baking trays and cook in a preheated oven, 190°C/375°F/gas 5, for 15–20 minutes or until the edges are just turning brown and the cookies are pale golden. Cool on racks. The cookies crisp up as they cool.

COLLEGE FOOTBALL PICNIC

This is serious sport. During the fall semester the big game of the season against the traditional rival university is very much an Old School Tie occasion, when old boys – and girls – travel thousands of miles to cheer on their team.

Fuelling this fervour demands warming food and drink. At the big games in the north-east, tailgate picnics served from the backs of those big American cars are likely to include thermoses of stiff drink to insulate the fans from the bitter cold, and a good chocolate cake to take up the slack.

BULLSHOTS

Bullshots are best served hot and peppery, and would do equally good service at point-to-points.

100ml strong beef
  consommé
50ml vodka
salt and freshly ground
  black pepper

serves 1

Heat the consommé in a saucepan. When it is just about to boil remove from the heat, add the vodka, salt and pepper, stir and pour into a thermos.

CRAZY CHOCOLATE CAKE

Crazy Cake is mixed, baked, iced and transported to the picnic all in the same tin. The ingredients and the method may seem a bit unusual but it really works.

225g self-raising flour
3 tablespoons cocoa powder
1 teaspoon bicarbonate of soda
225g sugar
pinch of salt
75ml sunflower oil
1 tablespoon cider vinegar
1 teaspoon vanilla extract
250ml cold water

TOPPING
115g unsalted butter, softened
115g brown sugar
1½ tablespoons double cream
75g walnuts, coarsely chopped

serves 8

1 Sift the flour, cocoa, soda, sugar and salt directly into a greased 20 x 20 x 5cm cake tin.

2 Make three egg-sized depressions in the dry mixture; into one pour the oil, into the next the vinegar, and into the third the vanilla. Pour the water over the top and beat with a wooden spoon until almost smooth and the flour is incorporated.

3 Bake in a preheated oven, 180°C/350°F/gas 4, for 30–35 minutes. Remove and cool in the tin for 10 minutes, but do not turn off the oven.

4 To make the topping, beat the butter, sugar and cream to a thick paste; spread on top of the warm cake, scatter over the walnuts and return to the oven for 3 minutes.

5 Leave to cool. Cut into squares and serve.

THANKSGIVING DAY

The Pilgrim Fathers, who braved the sea crossing in the seventeenth century from England to the New World, were better sailors than farmers. The seeds and plants they brought with them did not flourish in the harsh climate of what is now New England. Had the local Indian tribes not offered shelter from the bitter winter, and help with the spring planting of native crops, the Pilgrims would have perished. But, after that first successful harvest, they celebrated with a feast of Thanksgiving, and it was to the Indians as well as to the Lord that they gave thanks. Thanksgiving, on the last Thursday in November, is celebrated in New York with a colourful parade along Central Park West. My family lived on the route and there was always a breakfast party for family and friends who came to cheer the marchers from the wide balcony.

left Macy's Thanksgiving Day Parade; Thomas A. Kelly/Corbis
above Pilgrims and Turkey Float at a Thanksgiving Day Parade; Kelly-Mooney
Photography/Corbis

CORNBREAD STUFFING FOR A TURKEY

115g butter, diced
500g cornbread, crumbled
280g soft breadcrumbs,
  white or wholemeal
115g bacon dripping or butter
150g walnuts, chopped
  (optional)
125g celery, diced
1 medium onion, finely
  chopped
1 green pepper, deseeded and
  finely chopped
2 teaspoons salt
freshly ground black pepper
½ teaspoon each of thyme,
  marjoram and sage
small bunch of parsley,
  chopped
2 large eggs, beaten
250–600ml turkey (or chicken)
  stock

makes enough to fill the cavity
of a 5.5kg bird for traditional
Thanksgiving dinner

1 Mix the butter, cornbread and breadcrumbs in a large bowl.

2 Heat the dripping or butter in a frying pan, add the nuts (if used), celery, onion and green pepper and sauté slowly for 5 minutes.

3 Add to the cornbread mixture with the salt, pepper and herbs, mixing thoroughly.

4 Add the eggs and gradually mix in the stock, stirring gently until the stuffing is of the desired consistency, and not too sloppy.

5 Stuff lightly in the neck and body cavity of the turkey. If there is any left over spread it in a greased ovenproof gratin dish and bake for 30 minutes or until crisp on top.

CRANBERRY-ONION CONSERVE

A delicious alternative to the usual cranberry sauce, this conserve is excellent with game and terrines as well as the inevitable cold turkey.

60ml olive oil
900g sweet onions, thinly sliced
8 garlic cloves, minced
50ml cider vinegar
3 tablespoons brown sugar
450g cranberries
salt and freshly ground black
    pepper to taste

makes about 1 litre

1 Heat the oil in a wide, deep frying pan, add the onions and the garlic and cook on a high heat, without stirring, for 5 minutes. Stir the onions and continue cooking, on medium heat, stirring occasionally to prevent burning, until they reach a deep glossy brown.

2 Add the vinegar, the brown sugar and the cranberries. Stir well and continue cooking on medium heat until the cranberries have dissolved, the mixture is thick, surplus liquid from the onions and the cranberries has evaporated and the fruit is soft. Add salt and pepper to taste.

3 Pack in clean, warm jars, seal and keep in the fridge for up to three months.

MOLASSES-GINGERNUT MUFFINS

For tender, light muffins, carefully stir rather than beat the mixture. You can also make this into a wonderful ginger cake, in which case you will need to use a well-greased loose-bottomed 25cm cake tin.

225g unsalted butter
350g molasses/treacle
1 large egg
170g caster sugar
285g self-raising flour
1 teaspoon bicarbonate of soda
2 teaspoons ground ginger
1 teaspoon cinnamon
½ teaspoon grated nutmeg
pinch of ground cloves
grated rind of 1 orange
75g walnuts, coarsely chopped
75g preserved ginger in syrup,
    drained and chopped
115ml boiling water
75ml milk
walnuts and hazelnuts for
    topping (optional)

makes about 24 muffins

1 Melt the butter with the molasses in a small saucepan and set aside to cool.

2 Beat the egg and sugar in a large bowl until light and fluffy.

3 Sift the flour, bicarbonate of soda and spices and add to the egg mixture, alternating with the molasses and butter mixture.

4 Fold in the orange rind, walnuts and ginger. Stir in the water and milk.

5 Butter muffin- or bun-tins with 2cm wells. Fill each tin two thirds full. Bake in a preheated oven, 180°C/350°F/gas 4, for 20–25 minutes until brown and risen.

6 Leave to cool for 15 minutes in the tins. Serve warm, split and buttered. These muffins keep well and can also be frozen and reheated. Top with chopped nuts, if desired.

COLONIAL CHOCOLATE CHRISTMAS PUDDING

Dense, fruity steamed suet puddings were at one time quite usual in America. Early colonial manuscripts and receipt books gave instructions for hundreds of these sturdy confections, but after the middle of the nineteenth century they began to be replaced with lighter steamed sponge puddings. One Old Guard family who proudly trace their lineage to the Mayflower descendants, the Daughters of the American Revolution and the founders of the Naval Academy in Annapolis, Maryland, has served chocolate pudding at Christmas for as long as anyone can remember. The original recipe, from the 1840s, is still preserved with the family documents. Their chocolate pudding is as excellent today as it was in colonial days, and is still brought flaming to the table with a silver bowl of chilled Hard Sauce.

285g self-raising flour
170g dark brown sugar
3 tablespoons cocoa powder
1 teaspoon bicarbonate of soda
250ml buttermilk (or sour cream)
50ml melted butter
50ml brandy

serves 6

1 Mix the flour and the sugar in a bowl with your fingers to break up any lumps. Sift in the cocoa and bicarbonate of soda.

2 Mix together the buttermilk and melted butter and stir gently into the flour. Pour the mixture into a buttered 1.2-litre pudding basin. Cover with a double layer of pleated tinfoil (the pleat will allow room for expansion). Secure the foil with string and tie a handle over the top.

3 Steam, on a trivet, in 5cm of boiling water for 1 hour. Make sure you don't let the boiling water dry out; keep checking and top up if necessary.

4 Let the pudding stand in the basin for 10 minutes, then unmould onto a serving platter. Heat the brandy in a ladle, carefully set it aflame and pour it at once over the pudding as you bring it in.

HARD SAUCE

115g unsalted butter, softened
50ml double cream
170g brown sugar
40ml brandy

Beat the butter with the cream, adding the sugar a little at a time. When the mixture is light and fluffy, beat in the brandy until it is thoroughly absorbed. Serve chilled.